Plants

Flowers

Patricia Whitehouse

Heinemann Library
Chicago, Illinois

www.heinemannraintree.com
Visit our website to find out
more information about
Heinemann-Raintree books.

To order:
☎ Phone 888-454-2279
💻 Visit www.heinemannraintree.com
to browse our catalog and order online.

Edited by Adrian Vigliano and Harriet Milles
Designed by Joanna Hinton Malivoire
Picture research by Elizabeth Alexander
Originated by Heinemann Library
Printed in China by South China Printing Company Ltd.

13 12 11 10 09
10 9 8 7 6 5 4 3 2

Library of Congress Cataloging-in-Publication Data
Whitehouse, Patricia, 1958-
    Flowers / Patricia Whitehouse.
        p. cm. — (Plants)
Includes index.
Summary: Introduces the physical characteristics, life cycle,
and roleof flowers in the world of plants.
    ISBN 978 1 4109 3474 1 (HC), 978 1 4109 3479 6 (Pbk.)
    1. Flowers—Miscellanea—Juvenile literature. [1. Flowers.]
I. Title.
II. Plants (Des Plaines, Ill.)
    QK49 .W52 2002
    582.13—dc21
                                    2001003649

Acknowledgments
The author and publishers are grateful to the following for per-
mission to reproduce copyright material: Alamy pp. **4** (© Phil
Degginger), **12** (© M.Brodie), **16** (© PhotoStock-Israel), **18** (©
inga Spence), **19** (© Keith Glover), **21** (© Frank Blackburn);
Corbis p. **13** (© Frans Lanting); GAP Photos pp. **9, 23** (Dave
Zubraski), **10** (Andy Small); Photolibrary pp. **8, 23** (Christo-
pher Fairweather/Garden Picture Library), **11, 23** (Westend61/
Creativ Studio Heinemann); Science Photo Library p. **17**
(Geoff Kidd); Shutterstock pp. **5** (© Iuri), **6, 23** (© Pakhnyush-
cha), **7** (© Donald R. Swartz), **15** (© Kulish Viktoriia), **14** (©
SNEHIT), **20, 23** (© Tatiana Grozetskaya).

Cover photograph of a dahlia reproduced with permission
of GAP Photos Ltd./Marcus Harpur. Back cover photo of a
sunflower reproduced with permission of GAP Photos (Dave
Zubraski), and stem, Shutterstock (© SNEHIT).

We would like to thank Louise Spilsbury for her invaluable
help in the preparation of this book.

Every effort has been made to contact copyright holders of
any material reproduced in this book. Any omissions will
be rectified in subsequent printings if notice is given to the
publisher.

All the Internet addresses (URLs) given in this book were valid
at the time of going to press. However, due to the dynamic
nature of the Internet, some addresses may have changed, or
sites may have changed or ceased to exist since publication.
While the author and Publishers regret any inconvenience this
may cause readers, no responsibility for any such changes can
be accepted by either the author or the Publishers.

Contents

Some words are shown in bold, **like this**. You can find them in the Glossary on page 23.

What Are the Parts of a Plant?

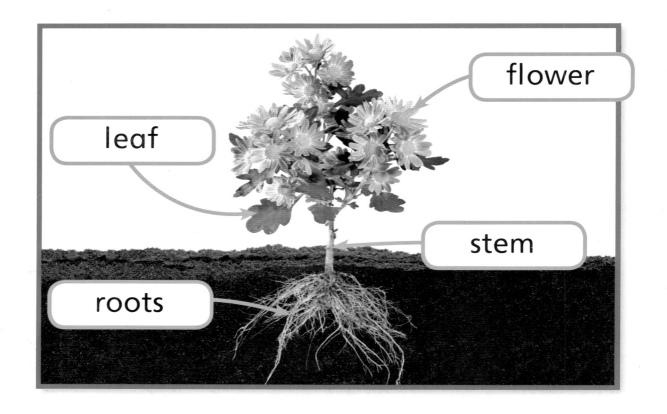

flower

leaf

stem

roots

There are many different kinds of plants.

All plants are made up of the same parts.

Some plant parts grow below the ground in the soil.

Flowers grow above the ground in the light.

What Are Flowers?

stem

Flowers are an important plant part.

They grow on the ends of **stems**.

Flowers grow on some trees, too.

These are the flowers on
cherry trees.

How Do Flowers Grow?

bud

Flowers grow inside **buds**.

Buds are flowers that have not opened yet.

petals

Buds need sunlight to open them up.

When a bud opens, you can see the colorful **petals** of the flower.

Why Do Plants Have Flowers?

seed

Flowers make **seeds**.

Seeds start to grow in the base of the flower.

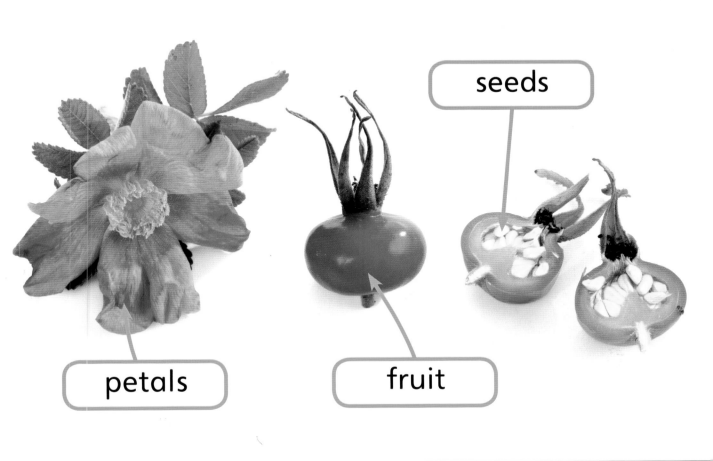

petals

fruit

seeds

The flower **petals** die and drop off.

Then a fruit grows with the seeds inside it.

How Big Are Flowers?

Flowers come in many sizes.

The forget-me-not in this picture is tiny.

Some flowers are very big.

The rafflesia is the biggest flower in the world.

How Many Flowers Can Plants Have?

Some plants have one flower.

Tulip plants grow a single flower at the top of their **stems**.

Some plants have many flowers.

The lilac plant grows hundreds of flowers at once.

What Do Flowers Smell Like?

Some flowers have a smell.

Many flowers smell nice.

These flowers smell horrible!

They are called skunk cabbage.

How Do People Use Flowers?

People use some flowers for food.

When you eat broccoli, you are eating flowers.

People use some flowers to make perfume.

People also give flowers as presents.

How Do Animals Use Flowers?

Some birds and insects use flowers for food.

They drink a sweet juice called **nectar** from the center of the flower.

Some insects and spiders hide inside flowers.

They can hide there because their color matches the flower.

Count and Record

This bar chart compares the number of petals on different flowers.

Can you see which type of flower has the most petals?

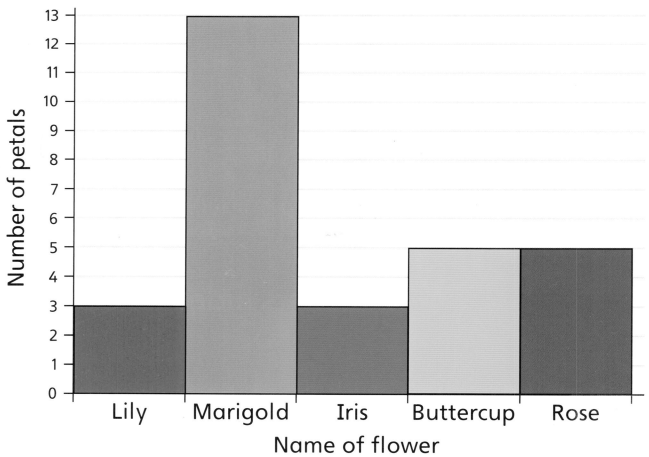

Glossary

 **bud** a flower or leaf that is still tightly closed

 **nectar** the sweet juice inside flowers that birds and insects like to drink

 **petal** the colored or white outer part of a flower

 **seeds** the part of a flower that new plants come from

 **stem** the part of a plant where the buds, leaves, and flowers grow

Index